We are all sailing on a ship that moves ahead with us every day. It is a ship with room to store all the treasures we find as we sail on and on and on. The ship is our life, and the treasures are the memories we store there for ourselves. Memories are not only for older people. Each one of us has memories. Each of us plans what we will do today and tomorrow. But when today and tomorrow are past, they are yesterday. And what happened on those days are memories. Memories can be magic. Unlike a computer that just gives back facts, memories bring back feelings, sounds, smells, pictures, laughter and tears. They can even keep us from repeating foolish mistakes—like eating too much chocolate cake, when we remember how sick three pieces made us the last time. The things we remember are our own story. Our memories are for special moments, to take out and enjoy ourselves, or to share with a friend.

Here are a few of my own very special treasures. I want to share them with you.

I was born on the other side of
the great Atlantic Ocean,
in the country of Austria
in the city of Vienna.

The earliest thing I remember is feeling snug and safe. My parents loved me.

When I was still very young, I remember going for a long vacation in the country, with my mother and my big sister. We wore dirndl dresses, which I liked. But we also wore white shoes, and I wore a big hat with a long feather. These I did not like very much.

When we came back to the city, we lived in a new apartment, with a ting-a-ling chandelier that made me think of a fairy palace. I also had a nice new dad with a moustache.

We could ride up to our apartment on an elevator. But we were supposed to walk down. When I stretched hard, I could push the button that would take us to our floor.

One morning my big sister took me into her bed and told me that she was going to get married. I knew that I would miss having her in our house. And I did.

But I was not without company. I had a friend who lived in the apartment building. Berta was the daughter of our super. We both liked to draw. Berta always drew dresses. I liked to draw people, especially sailors and places a sailor might go. Berta's brother was a sailor, so sometimes my pictures were of him.

When I was six years old, I started school. What I liked best was drawing and learning to read. Soon I was the fastest reader in the class.

Across from my apartment building was a store that sold small paperback books. I spent all my allowance there. I would buy one book, take it home and read it, then return it for another one. Sometimes in one afternoon I would read four books for the price of one.

At about the same time, I started taking dancing lessons with a famous dancer. I loved dancing. Our class began by dancing to a polonaise by Chopin, then did other group dances, waltzes and ballet. At the end of each lesson, we could each dance whatever we wanted to dance. Such joy! I felt as if I never wanted to stop dancing.

Our family always got together for Sunday dinner at one o'clock. After dinner, my dad and I would dance a czardas while my sister played the piano. My dad was Hungarian, and the czardas was a Hungarian dance.

Then I would dance an American dance with my brother-in-law. He was not an American, but he liked American dances. He was elegant, with shiny black hair. My sister said he wore a hairnet to keep his hair perfect.

Our cook was Hungarian, like my dad. We all loved her cooking. When she was through cooking, she took off her shoes and sat on the balcony near the kitchen. While she was resting, she told me stories about the village where she was born. I loved to listen to her.

I had a dog, two white rabbits and two birds as pets. I loved them very much.

When I came home from school one day, one of my birds looked different. I wanted to believe that it was the same Hansi. (All the birds were called Hansi.) But inside I knew that one of my birds had died and my mother had gotten me a new one because she didn't want me to be sad.

One day I became very ill. I was so sick that doctors came from everywhere to look at me, while I lay in bed. Some of their treatments hurt very much, but none of them helped.

I heard them say to my mother, "This child will die."

But my mother did not want me to die. She loved me too much. She stayed by my bedside night and day. And I did not die. It was her love that made me well again. My mother was beautiful, outside and inside.

During my illness, many people sent me flowers and plants. My favorite was something that looked like a skating rink (a mirror) with pine trees around and little figures skating.

I was sick for more than a year. I even had to learn to walk all over again. But finally I was ready to go back to school.

When I went to school, I did not know that I looked different. But I soon found out. The children pointed at me and laughed.

After I got home, I took a good look at myself. And I did look funny. My illness has left me with a crooked face. But my family loved me just the same, and I got used to looking different.

Crooked face and all, I sailed on to new things, good and bad, to store away with my remembered treasures.

I became very busy. I still liked reading and drawing. And I took piano lessons and French lessons. I started dancing lessons again, too.

My dancing went very well until I had to dance like a butterfly. I was supposed to go fluttering from flower to flower, from child to child. I was to bend down gracefully, then leap up quickly, as if I were flying. But once down, I could not get up. My legs were still too weak. I felt bad, and I cried.

Yes, I cried then.
But slowly I grew taller and stronger.
I also became an aunt.
My sister brought her baby boy to our Sunday dinners. During these visits he was put into my bed.
He never cried.

Because I wanted more money to buy books, I began to draw picture cards that I hoped to sell. The owner of the shop where I bought books said she would display them and pay me if she sold any. My dad was my first customer. But other people bought them, too. I felt proud.

I had a marvelous time going to art school. I felt quite grown up at life classes.

Of course, I wasn't grown up
enough to join my sister and
cousin, who were going
to a costume ball. Though
why they wanted to dress up
as children, I could not
understand. I thought
it would be much
more fun to dress
up in a beautiful
long gown.

It was always fun to be with my dad. He could blow the biggest smoke rings anyone ever saw. And he knew the names and the ancestors of all the race horses we saw when he took us to the races.

Every day, after he
closed his shop, my dad
would meet his friends
at his favorite coffee house.
A coffee house in Vienna
is a very special place.
When I was twelve years
old, he took my mother
and me there for frankfurters
with sweet horseradish.
I can still taste it. It was
wonderful. But best of all,
the coffee house had
magazines and newspapers
from all over the world
for everyone to look at and
read. Some I could understand,
others I could not. But as I
looked at them all, I knew that
MY WORLD was the best of all.

I was fourteen when a magazine first printed one of my drawings. Soon I was making a drawing every week for that magazine and also for a daily paper. My mother was so proud she called her best friend every time a picture appeared. My dad showed the magazine and paper to all of his friends at the coffee house. He was proud, too.

My world was wonderful.
I sailed ahead happily
collecting treasures
to remember.

Yet not all memories are good.
My dad got very, very sick.
He had been smoking
too much the doctors said.
And on a beautiful day, with
blossoms perfuming the
air (I can still smell them) and
birds chirping, he died.
I could not understand how
so much sadness could come
on such a joyous day.

Other things happened
that I could not understand
that year. A new leader and
a new order began to change
my world. Large groups
of people began to hate
other groups of people. If you
did not belong to the right
group, you and your family
could be destroyed.

One needed good luck to get away…

I was lucky. After a stopover at another country—
where I could even do drawings to support myself—
a big ship brought me to a fine new world.

I landed in New York no longer a child. Yet, like a child, I had to learn a new language and learn how to live in a new place. My sister and her son had arrived before me. My mother arrived two years later, but she lived for only a few weeks more.

Good or sad, everything one remembers is important. Our memories help make us the people we are. Each of us has different things to remember, different things to wonder about, different people to recall and to love.